Wayward Teen To Transformed Queen

STRATEGIES TO HELP YOUR TEENAGER SUCCEED

AN EIGHT STEP GUIDE FOR PARENTS OF
TEENAGE BOYS & GIRLS

SallyAnn Gray

Award-Winning Author & Educator

Wayward Teen to Transformed Queen

Copyright @ 2019 SallyAnn Gray.

All rights reserved. No part of this publication may be reproduced, stored in a retrieval system or transmitted in any form or by any means- electronic, mechanical, photocopying, recording, or any other- except for brief quotations in printed reviews, without the prior permission of the publisher. All scripture quotations are from the Holy Bible, King James or New International Version.

ISBN-13: 978-1-949343-54-0
ISBN-10: 1-949343-54-5
SallyAnn Gray Kingston, Jamaica

Illustrations by Mark Gray
Pictures by Mark Gray
Cover Design by Mark Gray
Edited by Fiona Burke
Printed in the United States

Visit us at www.SallyAnnGraySpeaks.com
Facebook: SallyAnnSpeaks
Instagram: @@SallyAnnSpeaks
Email: info@sallyanngrayspeaks.com

Proverbs 22:6 (KJV)

Train up a child in the way he should go: and when he is old, he will not depart from it.

Train up a child refers to the total process of molding a child's life. The word train (chanak) comes from the root word meaning to "put into the mouth," and implies the idea of conditioning the palate. Thus, parenting training should help children develop a taste for the things of God. **The Biblical pattern of effective parental training emphasizes balance of instruction and discipline**. The ideal parent is to neither be overly authoritarian nor overly permissive. **Rather, he must balance love and discipline so as not to 'provoke' his child to rebellion.** When he is old means simply, "when he is grown up," or a mature adult. It does not refer to elderly years. The verse stresses that education in the home forms the man throughout his lifetime.

The revelation God gave me is simply this: if there is a way children should go, then there is a way they should not. How we mold our children into choosing the right way is to be done at home in their childhood years, while we as parents yet still have influence over them.

DEDICATION

This book is dedicated to my two children. My son Malachi, who is eight, and my daughter Sarah, who is three. God chose me to be your mother and my commitment to you is to always raise you in the way you should go. My commitment is to train you in such a way that will cause you to develop a taste for the things of God. I stand on His promise that when you both get old and are no longer within the sphere of my influence, that you will not depart from your morals, values and guiding principles.

Mommy and Daddy love you both very much. You know what we stand for. Our commitment is to teach you about who God has called you to be. If we do not tell you, the world will, and that is not the will of God for you. You are chosen, set apart, royal and specially designed. You go and live out your God given purpose. You go and help as many people as you can. You go and do what you are called to do. Mommy and Daddy are living their purpose and that is what you should do too!

CONTENTS

Dedication..v

Acknowledgments...9

A Letter from My Parents to You..13

A Letter from Me to You...15

Introduction..19

Excerpt from "The Renewal"...21

CHAPTER 1 What Do You Know About Your Teenager?............25

CHAPTER 2 What Do You Desire for Your Teenager?...............37

CHAPTER 3 What Do You Believe About Your Teenager?........49

CHAPTER 4 What Are You Saying About Your Teenager?........57

CHAPTER 5 Who Is on Your Teenager Success Team?..............65

CHAPTER 6 What Is the Strategy for Raising Your Teenager?.77

CHAPTER 7 What Are You Modelling for Your Teenager?........87

CHAPTER 8 How Will You Fight?...95

ACKNOWLEDGMENTS

To the Holy Spirit, for revealing every word on every page, I say thank you; for without you, God's work could never be done in and through me.

To my husband Mark, you have been a source of strength and support from day one. Thank you for holding me down in life, in purpose and in our joint responsibility as parents. Thank you for being the voice of reason. I remember telling you when Malachi was only two, that he will attend Morehouse College in Atlanta because I always wanted my son, if I had one, to attend that college. I recall you telling me to relax and chill. "Sal, the boy is only two, give him a chance. What if that's not what he wants?" As parents sometimes this is what we do, we impose our dreams unto our children. Thank you for helping to keep me balanced on this journey. Let me pause here to say a huge thank you to your parents, Michael and Evelyn Gray, who did so well with you. Not only are you my husband, you are my friend. I like the person you are because you have a good and clean spirit; you are filled with character. Your parents showed you the way to go and it is evident now that you are a grown man.

To my beautiful children Malachi and Sarah, I have one favour to ask you. When you become teenagers, please ensure that I read this book every month. LOL. Seriously, Mommy commits to authenticity and integrity, therefore, whatever I am asking parents to do now with their teenage children, may I live it out when you get to this stage. I am asking you to hold me accountable to raise you, to love you, to train you and to guide you. I want you to know that I am not the perfect parent, but God knows we are perfect for each other. There is no other responsibility and role I take more importantly than my commitment to bringing you up in the admonition of the Lord. Thank you for loving me, you are my two precious gifts, and Mommy loves you so much.

To my loving and committed parents, Selburn and Marjorie Sharpe. Where do I start? Mommy and Daddy, I know I took you to hell and back as a teenager. I want to express how grateful I am for all the love you showered me with. To know I am not your child by blood, brings me to tears EVERY SINGLE TIME. You know why? Because I think about how much you love me, especially when I was hard to love. When everyone said I would never amount to anything, you guys stood by me. There are absolutely NO WORDS to describe the depth of my love and gratitude. **You both have SHOWED me the way, and for that I am grateful**. I salute you both because of who you are and what you both represent. Thank you for all you have done and continue to do.

A LETTER FROM MY PARENTS TO YOU

Dear Parents,

We know it is hard, we were once where you are today, but the good Lord is able. Develop a relationship with Him, because there may be some very dark nights that only He can help you out of.

If your teenager is out of control, get a support team in place. I cannot tell you how much the support of trusted friends helped prevent looming nervous breakdowns. Understand that you cannot share everything about your teenager with everyone. Look ONLY to trusted friends and people in your church family. Continue loving your child. Remember that like you, he/she is the image of God.

Usually, there is some underlying psychological reason why your teenager is acting out or behaving contrary to your expectations. It's usually not their fault. Seek professional help; Family Life Ministries is a great place to start. Keep track of your child's friends and monitor their social media accounts.

It might be a good idea to have social gatherings at your home. Invite your teenager's friends over to the house. This will help you get some insight into the mindset of the persons they are hanging out with.

Talk to the parents of all their friends. Compare and share notes with parents of other out of control teenagers. Always pray. Irrespective of what you see now, know that better can come from your teenage child.

Be encouraged. God turned it around for us, He will turn it around for you too!

Love always,
Selburn & Marjorie Sharpe,
Loving Parents to SallyAnn

A LETTER FROM ME TO YOU

Dear Parent,

Here is what I am NOT. I am not a child psychologist, I am not trained to handle or treat any kind of mental health issues and I am by no means a perfect parent myself. This book is not intended to degrade you as a father or mother, and it will NOT solve all the issues you face raising your teenager. I know that God has called me to write this book simply to help shift your mindset. Your relationship with your teenager can change right now if you shift your mindset.

Here is what I am. I am a trained special education teacher with over twenty years of experience teaching and dealing with students with special needs. I am an educational consultant who offers professional development for teachers. I help principals shift the mindset of their teachers, so they can experience more positive results with their students. I am a trained school inspector with the National Education Inspectorate of Jamaica. I am a curriculum designer who wrote special needs curricula for the Jamaican Government at HEART Trust/NTA for over five years. I have worked with the

Ministry of Education and in my last professional role, I was Head of School & Programmes Director for the TGL School of Sales & Sales Management at University of the Commonwealth Caribbean.

Here is what I was. I was adopted at three months old. My mother gave me to my adoptive parents when I was that young. When I found out at age eleven, it caused me to turn into a very rebellious child. I was a VERY rebellious teenager. I looked for love in all the wrong places. I did things to get the attention of others. It caused a lot of heartache for my parents. They took me from one doctor to the next, from one psychologist to the next, seeking help. I was eventually diagnosed with Attention Deficit Hyperactivity Disorder at the age of fourteen and I was kicked out of high school at the age of sixteen. I gave my parents countless headaches. I snuck out the house on many occasions to go to parties and other places. I stole things. I gave a lot of trouble. It was very embarrassing for them. I feel bad now and have asked for forgiveness, but at the time I had no clue about the implications of my behaviour. I did not understand how embarrassing it was for my parents or how much it hurt them. Your child may not be doing any of these things or they may be doing way more than I did as a teenager. **The point is, I stand as a representative of your teenager who may be rebelling and crying out for help.**

I was your teenager twenty years ago. And today, I represent who your child can be. All is not lost, Daddy. All is not lost, Mommy. All is not lost, Grandma. All is not lost, Caregiver. Whoever you are, if you are raising a teenager who is out of control in some way, this book is for you. **Even if your teenager is doing well, you can still benefit from this book. As parents, we can all improve and it is from this perspective, that I encourage all parents to take a read.** I am here to encourage you. I am here to share with you some strategies my mommy and daddy used with me. I am here to share with you some approaches I have used on my teenage students over the past twenty years, that have caused major shifts for them. I have been so blessed to witness tremendous transformation in teenagers dubbed the worst of the worst.

God did it for me, and He will do it for your child. I am passionate about helping you, because my parents experienced many challenges with me as a teenager. I was the child you would not want to raise, but today I am an adult my parents are proud of. I give GOD all the glory for my renewed mind and my transformed life.

With all the Love in My Heart,
SallyAnn Gray

INTRODUCTION

Parents, before jumping into the book, I wanted to give you a little background about my journey. I also want you to understand the reason behind why I do what I do. I thought it very fitting to share an excerpt from my first book with you. My first book is entitled **"The Renewal: Revive Everything Necessary Empower Within."** Please take some time to read an excerpt from Chapter 1- The Reason. As you read this excerpt, I ask that you reflect on your journey as a parent. What is your reason? What is your big why? Why is it important for your child to turn out a certain way? What can you adjust for this to happen? I pray that everything you read will penetrate your heart and shift your mindset as a parent.

EXCERPT FROM "THE RENEWAL"

For the vision is yet for an appointed time, but at the end it shall speak, and not lie: though it tarry, wait for it; because it will surely come, it will not tarry.

Habakkuk 2:3 (KJV)

To understand my reason, you have to understand my story. My biological mother gave me away at the age of three months. She was walking along a street in Kingston, Jamaica as she tried to get to a radio station. She wanted to make an announcement or ask someone to help her. She had a baby and was unable to care for her. As she walked toward the radio station, a man stopped his car and asked if she needed help or a ride. My biological mother made the decision to get in the car. As she explained her plight, the man revealed that he and his wife had been praying for a baby. Eventually, they came to an agreement, and she handed me over. That kind man and his wife became my parents.

As I grew older, my mom and dad explained the incidents that lead to them becoming my parents. I struggled as I tried to understand how a mother could give her child away to total strangers. It completely crushed my self-concept. It made me feel like I was not important. As a high school student, my low self-esteem morphed, and I became a wayward teenager. Many people told my mother I would never amount to anything in life. Despite the heart-breaking comments, my parents never gave up on me. They prayed hard, and with much intervention I was able to achieve academic and professional success.

During much of my adulthood, outward success masked the fact that there was little inner fulfillment. Some of the self-doubt and low self-esteem from my teenage years managed to resurface. I started to think about why these feelings were plaguing me so often. I asked God many times, is this it? Is this life? Work hard to pay bills, get home from work, feed the kids and go to bed? There just had to be more. My life had to have more meaning than this.

I started to realize that the fallacy presented to us as children to complete college, get a "good" and "stable" job, buy a house and live happily ever after, somewhat created an illusion of happiness and fulfillment for me. I was miserable despite having what appeared to others as the "perfect life". On the outside, others saw confidence, academic achievement, professional accomplishment, a happy marriage and two beautiful children. What I discovered, is that appearances serve as distractions from your true purpose. They help to create the illusion to everyone including you, that everything in your life is ok.

I realized that I was quickly growing sick and tired of the façade. I felt in the depths of my spirit that there was more for me to do. Misery was my best friend because I had not been walking in divine purpose. With all that emotional sickness, I had to get some medicine. When our physical man gets sick, we rush to the doctor for medication. When our spiritual man gets sick, we need to get medicine for the spirit.

End of Excerpt.

Parents, I asked that you reflect on your own life journey. Was there a time in your adult life when you pondered some of these same things? Do you ask, "What is my purpose?' Do you ever recall purpose being a topic of discussion when you were growing up?

I decided that I wanted to empower my children by speaking to them about both profession and purpose. I believe both have their place, I believe both are possible, and I believe both are necessary. Let us look at how we can shape the discussion in our homes to raise well rounded and balanced children. Children who will ultimately make life decisions based on a vision that aligns with God's ultimate purpose for their lives.

CHAPTER 1
WHAT DO YOU KNOW ABOUT YOUR TEENAGER?

- ✓ What do you THINK you know about your teenager?

- ✓ Do you really understand who your child is?

- ✓ Who have they become in this teenage season?

- ✓ Do you understand about their wants, their desires, their dreams, their purpose?

My husband always says to me, "Sal, I know you, so that did not surprise me." It always annoys me but it's so true. The best way to deal with people in general, and by extension teenagers is to get to know them. I mean, really understand them. Your sweet nine-year-old goes to bed one night and wakes up one morning, they are now fourteen, full of attitude, have a whole new personality and just like that, you must relearn them.

As a special education teacher who has taught both locally and internationally, I can tell you that there is one common thread among all teenagers. They just want to be understood and accepted for who they are.

First up on the checklist is, what do you think you know about your teenage child? List all the things you think you know about them below. What you think you know and the reality of who they are may shock you. This exercise is designed for you to start where you are, with the knowledge you have.

Below, I would like for you to take some time to reflect on what you THINK you know about your teenager. This exercise does not require you to have a conversation with them or anyone else. Just list out the things you THINK you know.

AS A PARENT I THINK I KNOW THESE THINGS ABOUT MY TEENAGER

_____
_____
_____
_____
_____
_____
_____

Wayward Teen to Transformed Queen

Once you have completed this exercise, I ask that you block some time to have a conversation with your child. Say to them, **"Mommy/Daddy wants to know as much as I can about who you are right now, I made some notes about who I think you are. Could you look at it with me and tell me if I am right?'**

NOTES BASED ON THE CONVERSTION

(DOCUMENT KEY POINTS FROM THE CONVERSATION)

_____
_____
_____
_____
_____
_____
_____
_____
_____
_____
_____
_____
_____
_____

Now that you have done the reflection and have had the conversation, how do you feel? Can you truly say you understand who your child is? Some parents may be spot on, but there might be a population of parents who are way off. The notion of truly understanding your child means everything to this process. The reason is this, when you know them, you can adequately plan for them. When you know them, you can tweak your approach. When you know them, you will not provoke them. When you take the time to truly know and understand them, it creates an opportunity for them to truly understand you and your concerns as a parent.

This brings me to another important point. I remember as a teenager, my mother hated when I wore black lipstick. If I was going to a party she would get extremely angry if I put that black lipstick on. The morning after I came home from a party, my mother came into my room and explained to me an incident with her aunt in her childhood that lead to her hating black lipstick. It was at this point I truly understood why. As a teenager, I felt compelled to never wear it again because my mother was open and honest about the reason behind it all.

Parents, by no means am I saying you should always have to explain away your decisions, by no means am I saying teenagers should always have their way. Discipline is

VERY important. What I am saying is, sometimes depending on their age and the lesson you are trying to teach, it may become necessary to have a heart to heart talk with your teenager. Explain to them using stories from your childhood, the reasons you may be trying save them from something. Try to develop that open and honest relationship of sharing with them.

Yes, I agree that boundaries have to be maintained because children should know they are children. As they mature into teenagers sharing openly will help. I guarantee it will make a difference. Let them know you had struggles growing up too and you want to help them make better choices and explain why. **Why is very important to teenagers**. It helps them connect. It also helps them to see that you are human. It helps them to understand you, and that is needed for your relationship to flourish.

Sometimes we try to love our children the way we receive love. Have you ever read the book entitled "The Five Love Languages" by Gary Chapman? In this book, Mr. Chapman highlights five specific love languages married couples use to relate to each other. The five love languages are: receiving gifts, quality time, words of affirmation, acts of service and physical touch. My two love languages are receiving gifts and words of affirmation. I made the mistake of thinking my children received love the same way I do. While they love gifts, I have grown to recognize that what is MOST important to them is quality time, especially my son Malachi. He values quality time a lot more than he does receiving gifts. I think it's important to evaluate the love language of our children so we love them how it matters to them most.

The key take away from this chapter is, you have to truly know your teen. Every step of the way. Every month there is a new trend, a new friend, a new interest, new issues, new likes and dislikes. If you hope to get your desired outcome as a parent, it is essential to shift your mindset to being open in every season. Its just the way teenagers are.

Chapter 1 Reflection

How do you feel about your current relationship with your teenager?

What could you do differently to improve your relationship?

What lessons have you learnt after reading this chapter?

CHAPTER 2
WHAT DO YOU DESIRE FOR YOUR TEENAGER?

- ✓ Your 'DESIRE' for them may change after you get to know and understand them fully!

- ✓ Get clear around what you want!

- ✓ Create a vision for their life in **partnership** with them!

- ✓ They are not you and you are not them. It's their life, but you are mandated to love, train, guide and teach. How can this be done so everyone wins?

- ✓ How do you invite them into the conversation as a teenager so they can partner with you in creating a vision that works for both of you?

Desire is a funny thing. It can be great, and it can get a little dangerous as parents, when we DESIRE for our children to accomplish what we were not able to accomplish. With the best of intentions, we subconsciously want them to pick up where we left off in school, in sports, in purpose and in so many other areas. When this does not align with the desire they have for their own life, there is a struggle and great conflict.

Take for example, a father who was on his way to becoming a football star athlete in high school. Let's say for argument sake, he was injured and was unable to live out his dreams of becoming the star player. He is now determined that his son will follow his footsteps and realize the dream he once had for himself. This is great if his son desires to be a football star himself.

The struggle becomes evident when this teenage boy has a different desire for his life. He may be good at playing football but does not desire for this to be a career for himself. What can happen here, is that, he may share it with his father and be met with opposition. Or he may not share, and feel as though he is under tremendous pressure to live up to the expectations of his father. Can you see how this may cause conflict? Can you see how this son may start resenting his father? Can you see how this resentment may lead to him displaying some undesirable behaviours? The point is, when a child, especially a teenager is acting out, there is ALWAYS a root cause. My encouragement is to get to the root cause of the conflict.

Always try to uncover the root cause of the underlying behaviour?

It is natural as parents for us to have a vision for the life of our children. As they mature, get older and start their teenage journey they start to develop a desire for their own life. They start to have things they want to do which may be completely opposite to what we had desired for them. It is essential at this point that we have consistent and meaningful conversations with teenagers and invite them to collaborate. **YES, as parents it is your job to guide and train, not own and rule**. At some point we will have to come to terms with the fact that it is their life. What I am encouraging here is collaboration and bargaining.

This is where we bridge both worlds. Your world and their world must become one for the collaboration to take place. Meaning, you as the parent have to understand that they are growing up in a very different era. They have a lot on their plate or so they think. In our minds, as parents we are thinking "wait until you have two bills to pay and you will understand real problems." To them, the problems they face as teenagers, be it friendships, acceptance, fitting in and self-esteem are HUGE in their eyes. They do not yet understand that life is more than friends, partying and being part of the in crowd. What I am asking you to do here, parents, is try to understand where they are coming from.

Lets say you have a dream for your child to attend university. They on the other hand do not see university as a priority, they see it as a waste of time. It may be necessary at this point to show them what a high school graduate earns in comparison to a university graduate. Speak to them by showing the end result or implications of their decision and let them know that ultimately it is their decision.

Outside of what you want them to become, get clear on **WHO** you want them to become. For example: to be responsible, able to make sound decisions, be well-rounded and valuable contributing members of society. Focusing on who you want them to become helps to shift the focus from lawyer and doctor as the outcome. Rather, we free ourselves to focus on the intangible attributes that will ultimately take them through life. I think fundamentally we all want our children to be whole, we want them to have a good heart, we want them to treat people well, we want them to help others. And yes, we want them to be able to earn and take care of themselves. So as we look at how to strike the balance as parents, let us involve them in the journey. Always explaining to them why it is important to us that they evolve into well rounded human beings.

Occasionally, I think it is important to ask yourself the following questions:

- ✓ **What is my child's purpose?**

- ✓ **What were they born to do?**

- ✓ **Is it my responsibility to help them uncover their purpose?**

- ✓ **How can I help/support them in their purpose work?**

Profession is very important, because as parents, we have a responsibility to ensure they can earn and take care of themselves. Purpose on the other hand is their life's work. It is what God has called them to do. That is extremely important. That said, as parents, our number one task is to be in prayer for our children. Asking God daily, by the minute and by the hour, to show us His purpose for their life so we can nurture it. Parenting does not come with a manual, which is why we look to our maker for insight and follow the word of God as we seek to train our children.

As you reflect on the information shared in this chapter, take some time to answer these questions:

What qualities do you want your teenager to have?

What profession would you like them to study for? Is it the same as what they want for themselves?

Is it possible to partner with them on what the vision should look like?

_____

_____

_____

_____

_____

_____

_____

_____

_____

What needs to happen for this to become a reality in your home?

_____

_____

_____

_____

_____

_____

_____

_____

_____

List the next steps you need to take as a mother or father or collectively, that will create a VISION for your teenager that is in alignment with God's purpose for their life.

NEXT STEPS

1

2

3

4

Wayward Teen to Transformed Queen

Chapter 2 Reflection

What did you learn from this chapter?

CHAPTER 3
WHAT DO YOU BELIEVE ABOUT YOUR TEENAGER?

- ✓ Do you really believe that they are beautiful/handsome, capable and deserving of every good thing?

- ✓ Do you really believe that they can and will change?

- ✓ Do you TRULY believe that a day is coming when you will get over this challenge?

We have heard the saying "belief kills and belief cures." It is true, and it also applies to what you truly believe about your teenager in any season of their life. Irrespective of what you may be faced with now, your level of belief and your posture determines everything right now. If your child is anything like who I was, it may be difficult to keep believing and remain positive. As a mother now, I reflect on what my parents were thinking on that fateful day when they were called to a meeting at my high school to hear these words, "Mr & Mrs. Sharpe, we believe Sally would benefit from a different environment." Can you imagine the shock, the horror and the disappointment? As a parent, if your child is kicked out of high school, it is easy to start thinking about all the things that may not become a reality for them.

Parents, all I can say is this: God is real. Hold your position. Pray and remain focused on the PROMISE. The enemy will try to get you off track. He will even convince you that your child will not amount to anything. Parents, PRAY and HOLD YOUR POSITION! BELIEVE what you know in your heart about YOUR child. Know that this too shall pass. Know that change can and WILL come. A day is coming when you will look back and smile and say, "Lord, I thank you!"

What has God promised you about your child?

_____
_____
_____
_____
_____
_____
_____
_____

Did you get any prophecy about who they will become? What was it?

_____
_____
_____
_____
_____
_____
_____
_____
_____
_____

How often do you pray about it?

_____
_____
_____
_____
_____
_____
_____
_____

How often do you communicate the promise to your child?

Parents, just a quick tip here. I am encouraging you to always speak about who your child WILL BECOME. Speak to who they have been ordained to be. Speak it in their presence and out of their presence. Remind them of who they are and who they have been called to be! Make it a daily practice!

Remember, out of the abundance of the heart the mouth speaks. Therefore, this chapter addresses what you believe in your heart about your teenager, first. What you believe in your heart, will roll off your lips. As a parent, you have to be conscious of that and sensitive to the effects it will have on your children. Speak what you want to see and do not speak what you are currently experiencing.

Chapter 3 Reflection

Now that you have read this chapter, do you have any new commitments to your teenage child?

_____
_____
_____
_____
_____
_____
_____

What will you be intentional to believe about who they are NOW and who he/she will be in the future?

_____
_____
_____
_____
_____
_____
_____
_____

CHAPTER 4
WHAT ARE YOU SAYING ABOUT YOUR TEENAGER?

- ✓ What are you saying about them and to them?

- ✓ What is your daily declaration over your teenager?

- ✓ The power of parenting is great when we speak life into our children even when the situation looks dead!

Now that we have addressed the posture of our heart and what we truly believe, now we can focus on the words we speak. The entire world was formed out of a series of spoken words. Let there be light, and there was _____? Yes, that's correct, light followed after the spoken command.

I think it is very important to apply this principle to our teenage children. We speak what we know and believe irrespective of what we are seeing them do now. Irrespective of the decisions they make now, we speak what we KNOW. Our words do in fact have the power to create and shape the lives of our children. The sooner we shift our mind around that, the sooner we will experience the freedom that comes with knowing we can literally breathe life into them right now.

I used to say how miserable my daughter Sarah is. Did you know what I noticed? Just how miserable she became even seconds after me uttering those words! I have now started to declare how sweet she is, I have started to declare how patient she is, and I have started to declare how at peace she is. Honestly, I can see these qualities coming through, even a little. I am going to keep praying, keep declaring and holding my position. I have decided to be conscious of what I speak into her life and into the life of my son Malachi, and I am encouraging you to do the same.

If you know anything about me, you will know that Priscilla Shirer is one of my favourite authors, ministers and speakers. About a year ago, I was watching an interview with her on TBN, where she shared that she speaks some DAILY DECLARATIONS over her three boys. I found it interesting. She stated in the interview that it was her responsibility to tell her children who they were, because if she did not, the world would.

I cannot tell you how profound this statement was to me. Most importantly, after hearing her approach, I sprung into action and wrote some declarations for my own children, which I will share with you. The most important lesson here, is that I sprung into action. Parents, reading this book is great and getting advice and tips from others about how to help your teenager is all good too. All I ask, is that after doing your due diligence and getting some good tips, you take action. There is no point in acquiring knowledge if there is no action applied to it.

I am encouraging you to write some daily declarations to speak over your teenager, as a matter of fact, its for all your children. Young, old and in-between. Let us work together and help to create a future for our children we can be proud of, by speaking only what we want to see. It works; I know it works because my mother always said, "I know she will amount to something," and "I know you will do well." Now she is seeing the fruit of that spoken word, and you will too.

Below are the daily declarations I speak over my children. Now, I also allow them to speak it over themselves. I am believing God that nobody will be able to turn them into followers because I have already declared them leaders and most importantly, they have declared it over themselves.

Daily Declarations For Malachi & Sarah

I am the head and not the tail

I am a leader and not a follower

I am fearfully and wonderfully made

I am a child of God

I am free from ALL generational curses

I am a blessing to my teachers and friends

I always retain what I learn

I do great things for the Kingdom of Jesus Christ

I show love and I have joy

I am at peace and I show kindness

I am patient and show goodness

I am gentle and full of faith

I am healthy and my body is free from disease

I am rich in all areas of my life

I have self-control and

God loves me!

As a mother, I cannot see a mile down the road. I do not know exactly how things will turn out with my children. I imagine I will have my share of questions when they become teenagers. I definitely will not get everything right, but I am committed to ensuring that I do what I can. What I can do NOW, is speak life into them and PRAY for them.

All I ask of you, Parents, is that you do the same. You may not have been doing this when your child was young, but you can start now. If you are asking the question, what can I do now? What do I have control over right now? This is it! You can change what you say. Just like that: and it is free. It does not require any external help. You can choose to speak only what you want to see. You can choose to declare, even in the hardest moments, that you expect only God's best for your teenage daughter or son.

We will not settle! I am right here on the journey with you. I need you to do it because I may need you to remind me when Malachi and Sarah become teenagers and the pressure hits. I may need you to say, "Sally, remember your own words in this little book." It's not easy, but it is necessary. Let's all commit to doing what is necessary for our children, teenage or otherwise. What is necessary and very important, is what we say to them and what we say about them.

Chapter 4 Reflection

I am not asking you to have this conversation with anyone else, all I ask is that you reflect on some of the things you have said about your child. Have they all been positive and encouraging? If not, I ask that you think about how you can speak about your teenager in a way that will build him or her up.

What are some things you are resolute about speaking over your teenager now?

_____
_____
_____
_____
_____
_____

Write your personal Daily Declaration for your teenager:

_____
_____
_____
_____
_____

Tip: You may consider printing it and pasting it on the wall in your room and your child's room. I have done that. I also ensure they say it every morning before they leave the house and I try my best to declare it over them consistently. I want to constantly remind them about who God says they are.

CHAPTER 5
WHO IS ON YOUR TEENAGER SUCCESS TEAM?

- ✓ Who are you sharing with?

- ✓ Who is on your team?

- ✓ Who has the best interest of your child at heart?

- ✓ Are you sharing with people who do not need to know?

You cannot raise your child alone. You need help. A support system is necessary. One thing I can say about my parents is, they had every person in the church praying for me. Who I am today is in direct alignment with those prayers. I am also a product of all the help my mother solicited. She did not sit in silence. She spoke to people (experts) who could give tips on how I could be helped. After I was diagnosed with Attention Deficit Hyperactivity Disorder (ADHD), my mother went into full gear. I have two aunts who are nurses and my mother sought their help about the best medication for me. Instead of rushing to place me on the first set of medication that was prescribed, she sought help from a team of persons.

Your teenager may not have been diagnosed with any disability. The problem may not be that severe; the point is, whatever the issue you are facing, speak to highly qualified people who have KNOWLEDGE, EXPERIENCE and EXPERTISE about that issue.

My mother shared with me when I got older, that she had to be very careful who she shared my issues with because some people were not listening to help. There were some people who were listening just to further discuss the matter and turn it into an unnecessary soap opera. Share only with people you are sure have a pure interest in HELPING your teenager overcome this hurdle and be better.

This may not always be the people at work, in your church or family members either. Pray for discernment and watch the actions of people. **Understand that not every EAR wants to help**. I would like to underscore the importance of raising your teenager in church. Believe you me, I know that there are churches and pastors out there who may not do right by their members. Equally, there are many good churches out there. Good men and women of God, who have made it their life's mission to pour into the development of families.

I have had the distinct pleasure of being associated with three such churches in my lifetime. The church where I was raised and first baptized at age fourteen, was Tarrant Baptist Church located in Kingston, Jamaica. At that time, the church was under the leadership of Rev. Neville Callam. My mother was a member there and she had everyone at that church praying for me. I can say that even though I gave a lot of trouble, there were some things I would not do. The reason for this, is the teachings I got in Sunday school while there.

The second church I have been a member of, is Emanuel Baptist Church located in Summerville, South Carolina. I was an adult teaching in South Carolina when I joined this church. By this time, I had my own two children and was happy to be under the leadership of a man of God who understands the value of family and raising children in the ways of the Lord. This church is led by Pastor John T. Miller and Lady Wanda Miller who taught my husband and me the importance of family and how parents must lead by example. My husband and I got re-baptized in this church and we have seen the positive effects on our children. We SHOW the way as opposed to just telling the way.

I have now moved back to Jamaica and joined Go for God Family Church led by Pastors Christopher and Marsha Morgan. This church focuses on building strong families. I can tell you that I have seen the benefits of the children's ministry on my children.

What I can say about all the three churches I have been affiliated with thus far, is that they are Bible based, seeking after God and most importantly, modelling what they hope to see in their members.

As you consider who you would like to have on your teenager success team, may I suggest, if you do not already have one, A CHURCH HOME. Who do you worship with? Who are you praying with? Who are you sharing with? If you are experiencing challenges with your teenager, I am not saying the church can solve all your problems, all I am saying is, there are benefits that come with being under the covering of a ministry. There are some benefits that come from membership within a church family. One is this, you have a haven where you can discuss with your pastor the issues you are facing and get prayer and some actionable help.

I understand this may not be the case in your situation. Maybe you had a bad experience at a church. I guarantee you, there are still good churches and good pastors out there, and when you find one, it does make a difference. My parents kept me in church and while it did not seem to work at the time, I am living proof that God's word NEVER returns to Him void.

In addition to a church family, I also encourage you to share with God parents, aunts and uncles who have an interest in the success of your teenager. What about your doctor? Maybe a psychologist or a trained counsellor? Depending on the issue at hand, you may need to get these persons on your team. It may also be useful to speak with the guidance counsellor at their school.

Ultimately, you want to exercise good judgement, use discernment and ensure that the people you have on the team all have one thing in mind, which is the success of your teenager. If you have someone on the team now who is only causing confusion and adding to any existing chaos, get rid of them.

What qualities are you looking for in these team members? They should be loving, kind, caring yet still frank and upfront. They should be supportive of where your teenager is heading and the vision you have for them. Ultimately, you want an objective and supportive cheerleader who can hold you down in some serious prayer. **Most importantly, they must know you and**

your child. You may also want someone who understands children and how they think. A sound and experienced educator would be a good choice.

As you reflect on your **TEENAGER SUCCESS TEAM**, I ask that you think about who needs to be on this team.

As you seek to coach your teenager to success, why is a team even necessary?

_____
_____
_____
_____
_____
_____
_____

List the persons on your **TEENAGER SUCCESS TEAM** and indicate why they are a part of the team. Please include yourself and indicate your purpose on the team as well. Each member must be adding value to the life of your teenager.

MEMBERS OF THE TEAM

Team member 1

Name: _____

Reason for choosing this person:

_____

_____

_____

Purpose they will serve on the team:

_____

_____

_____

Team member 2

Name: _____

Reason for choosing this person:

_____

_____

_____

Purpose they will serve on the team:

_____

_____

_____

Team member 3

Name: _____

Reason for choosing this person:

_____
_____
_____

Purpose they will serve on the team:

_____
_____
_____

Team member 4

Name: _____

Reason for choosing this person:

_____
_____
_____

Purpose they will serve on the team:

_____
_____
_____

Team member 5

Name: _____

Reason for choosing this person:

_____
_____
_____

Purpose they will serve on the team:

_____
_____
_____

Team member 6

Name: _____

Reason for choosing this person:

_____
_____
_____

Purpose they will serve on the team:

_____
_____
_____

Team member 7

Name: _____

Reason for choosing this person:

_____

_____

_____

Purpose they will serve on the team:

_____

_____

_____

Now that the team is in place, ensure that you have a conversation with each team member. Let them know you value the contribution they can make and you are officially asking for their help with the issue at hand.

You can now decide how you provide updates and how you solicit their help. Whatever you are struggling with, ask for help. You cannot do it alone.

Chapter 5 Reflection

Have you been sharing with the wrong people?

_____
_____
_____

Do you believe the formation of this team will help you as you coach your child to success?

_____
_____
_____

CHAPTER 6
WHAT IS THE STRATEGY FOR RAISING YOUR TEENAGER?

- ✓ Sammy and Sally are two different teenagers.

- ✓ **What is an Individualized Success Plan (ISP)?**

- ✓ How do I write one?

- ✓ Review the template!

- ✓ When is a good time to implement the ISP?

- ✓ My pledge to be CONSISTENT in its execution!

Teenagers will have you going in circles. Between the hormones and the attitude, they could keep you guessing for years to come. I know parents who have two teenagers in the house. Some of whom made the mistake to assume that what worked with one will work with the other. I am here to tell you that the approach that worked with Sammy (child A), may or may not work with Sally (child

B). Further to that, approaches that work with boys, may not necessarily work with girls. What does this mean for you as the parent? Well, it means you will have to know your child, you will have to understand your child and you will have to plan for your child individually.

As a special educator, I have spent the better part of the last twenty years writing Individualized Education Plans (IEP's) for my teenage students with special needs. Even though students are grouped according to disability, there is still a need to create a PLAN that is individualized for each child. The IEP would take into consideration present levels of performance and look at where the team wanted the student to be by the end of the school year. The team would carefully craft some goals the child was most likely to accomplish based on all the evidence and present levels of performance.

What I am suggesting in this chapter is a similar concept. If you hope to coach your child to success, you cannot wish and hope for it. You must plan, strategize and execute. So, what is an ISP? It is an **Individualized Success Plan (ISP)**. This plan must be different for each teenage child you have. Why? Every child is different. Every child has different desires, interests, wants, passions and a different purpose. The team members for each teenage child may be different, and the goals will be different as well.

Here are some frequently asked questions about the ISP:

What are the components of an ISP?

The **ISP** will document the vision for the life of your teenager (Be flexible, things can and will change. The plan can be adjusted.)

It will include vision, goals, action steps, resources and persons responsible for each action item

It will also include timelines

It is important to note that all of these can be tweaked as you learn more about your teenager and as seasons change. But it is important to have something. How can you help them get somewhere when you do not know where they are going?

What does it look like?

It is a one to two-page document; very simple yet detailed. Actual templates will be provided further in the book that you can use. Feel free to tweak as you see fit.

Who will complete it?

The entire team, to include your teenage child, will be responsible for completing it. As an educator, I have witnessed many parents planning for their children, but they neglected to include the most important person-the child. While I agree that children should not be privy to every conversation, I believe in their teenage years, they can be given a healthy level of autonomy to weigh in on their passion, their dreams and their purpose. It is after all, their life. Our role is to guide and advise. Parents have the wisdom. Teenagers have the desire. Therefore, collaboration is needed.

Who will update it?

Updates ideally should take place with the team. At the very least, parents and teenager should be present.

Does your child really need to be a part of it?

They absolutely should! I believe it is very healthy for teenagers to have a say in the decisions that are about to affect their adult years.

INDIVIDUALIZED SUCCESS PLAN (ISP)

Name: _____

Age: _____

OVERALL VISION

Goals	Action Steps	Resources Needed	Persons Responsible	Timeline

Below I offer a brief explanation of the information required for each column. Additional pages with the ISP template will be provided for your use and reference at the back of the book.

OVERALL VISION

What is the overall vision for the life of your teenage child? What is their purpose? For you to guide your child to a destination, you will have to know where it is. In this section, document the vision for their life.

GOALS

The goals outlined for your teenager must be SMART (Specific, Measurable, Actionable, Realistic & Timebound).

ACTION STEPS

Each identified goal will require action for it to be achieved. List at least three actionable steps the team can do NOW to move the goal closer to attainment. Update and keep adding action steps until the goal is achieved.

RESOURCES NEEDED

For the goal to be achieved, resources may be needed. In this column, list all the resources that are required for the goal to be achieved. The team can then strategize around how these resources can be obtained.

PERSONS RESPONSIBLE

In Chapter Five, we discussed ideal team members for your Teenager Success Team. In this column, list team members who are accepting responsibility to help with something towards the achievement of an identified goal.

TIMELINE

Goals without timelines are just a wish. As a parent, do not get into the practice of wishing for your teenager. Do not wish; WORK. For every identified goal, there must be an achievement date. After discussing as a team, decide on a reasonable timeline.

I would like to take the time here to say it is absolutely necessary to make changes and tweaks to this document, so it makes sense for your teenager. Also, understand that the plan will not jump off the page and accomplish itself. Everyone on the success team has to do their part, including your teenage child. Now is as good a time as any to remind them that it is their life and ultimately you can plan along with them, but they also have a BIG role to play. After you have done all you can do, in the end, the choices your child makes will mould their life and create their reality.

Therefore, it is extremely important to raise your child in the way they should go. Help them to develop a palate for certain things when they are young. When they get to the teenage stage, you will not have to force them into completely unfamiliar territory. Consequently, it is important to determine who we want them to become, before deciding what they will become. As parents, I think if we decide on WHO we want them to become very early, WHAT they will become can be trained in a much easier way.

CHAPTER 6 REFLECTION

How do you feel about the Individualized Success Plan (ISP)?

_____
_____
_____
_____
_____
_____
_____
_____

Do you think it will help you better coach your teenager toward success? If yes, why? If no, why?

_____
_____
_____
_____
_____
_____
_____
_____

CHAPTER 7
WHAT ARE YOU MODELLING FOR YOUR TEENAGER?

- ✓ What are you doing and what are they observing?

- ✓ Understanding the hidden curriculum!

- ✓ Indirect values, morals and attitudes!

I am a mother too and this is the part I really hate to hear, but it is necessary for me to face. Some of my behaviours both good and bad, are being observed by my children. So parents, here is the hard truth: we are not perfect. We cannot be, nor will we ever be. Now that we are clear on that, how can we honestly face ourselves when we observe some very undesirable behaviours in our children we know they picked from us?

This is a touchy subject and I am right there with you. I am not happy to be the bearer of this news either because sometimes I step out of line as a parent. So how do we navigate this space? Is it fair to say we should have a conversation with our teenage children about our failures, our anxieties and why we do or do not do certain things? Will this conversation change anything for them? Will it influence their behaviour if we allow them to see our authentic and vulnerable side? In the times when we do mess up as parents, the times when we know we are guilty of displaying a negative behaviour we now see our child displaying, what should we do? You know that moment? The moment when we truly have to parent ourselves out of our own child. What happens then?

For me, I think it's a neat balance. Having taught difficult teenagers over the past twenty years, I can guarantee that you do not want to tell them everything. In some instances, it depends on the situation, the lesson you are trying to teach and their maturity level.

What I hope to provide in this chapter is AWARENESS. Just be open and honest so you may walk in the freedom of awareness as parents. For with awareness you can now choose. You can be more conscious of what you do around them; the attitudes you display around them. When I tell my son Malachi no sweets after 8:00 pm, he very quickly reminds me of all the times he has observed me having a bowl of Devon House ice-cream way after 8:00 pm. I was not very amused and pondered on how to get out of the double standard scenario I had created.

In education, there is something referred to as the hidden curriculum. The hidden curriculum is the values, attitudes and behaviours students subconsciously pick up from their teachers. They are learned but not openly intended. The transmission of norms, values and beliefs conveyed in the classroom and the social environment. It is what a student learns from their teacher by observing them over a period. For example, a teacher may never say to his/her students, you must be on time for class, but the teacher may display the value he/she places on punctuality by consistently showing up early for class. Indirectly, over the period of that school year, the students learn whose class they must be punctual for and whose they can be late for. All this, simply by the behaviour and pattern created by the teacher over time.

As parents, we must also examine the hidden curriculum within the home. The values, attitudes and morals we subconsciously transmit to our children without saying a word. I remember observing my father greet EVERY single person he came across on the street by saying, "Good morning." All the way from the security guard to the CEO. Now as an adult, I cannot help but say, "Morning" as I pass people. Subconsciously, I picked it up and now it is a part of me.

As you reflect on your journey as a parent, what values and attitudes have you unknowingly displayed that your teenager has subconsciously picked up? You never once opened your mouth and said, "Be this way," or "Be that way." But now you see them being a certain way or displaying behaviours you know they have adapted from you.

This awareness was particularly enlightening for me. Matter of fact, it is not just applicable to teenagers but to all children. Armed with this awareness, how will you make some conscious changes to the behaviours you display? The truth is parents, for our children to get better, we must get better. We are their biggest influence. The family is where it all starts. We can blame the society, the teachers, the deejays, the pastor and the church but ultimately, they are our children; given to us to train and guide. What direction will they go in after they have observed you? After they have watched you live, what kind of person will they be inspired to be?

I can honestly say that much of who I am now is a combination of what was said to me by my parents, along with how they lived. I will never forget observing my parents help countless children in the neighbourhood where I grew up. My mother taught so many children how to read. My father helped so many young boys by paying them to cut the yard if they needed money. They served in church, they were always stretching their hands, but always to give. Subconsciously I picked that up. They never really taught me a lesson on giving. They lived kindness and compassion. I am so ever grateful to them for how they lived. The hidden curriculum in my home has shaped who I am.

The biggest lesson I learnt from how my parents lived, is grace. I am not the birth child of my parents and even after taking them to hell and back during my teenage years, I always knew I was their daughter. Even after sneaking out the house a hundred times, I always knew I could go back home. They never spoiled me. They were always firm and always disciplined me, but somehow, I always knew there was grace. There was something about the compassion they displayed not only to me, but to others. It is that compassion that has kept me grounded, kept me humble and kept me solid.

When its all said and done, as parents, we all want well rounded, well adjusted contributing members of society as our off spring. In the end, it won't matter so much what their profession is: lawyer, doctor, indian or chief. What will matter most is who they are. The essence of their spirit. Who they helped and the legacy they will leave behind.

Whether you believe it or not parents, whether you embrace it or not, we have a HUGE role to play in that. Let us lead them not only in words but in deeds. For what we do will have a much bigger impact than what we say.

If we want them to be loving, we must show them love and display it to others. If we want them to be kind, we must be kind and show them kindness. If we want them to be respectful, we must show them and others respect. That is SHOWING them the way to go. Saying and living must go hand in hand. A delicate balance of love and discipline is essential, and during their teenage years, it is very crucial.

As parents, it is essential to have a vision for them. When they become teenagers, we invite them to collaborate with us. We have to truly explain our role in their lives. We have to show them how God designed for us to train them. We must also teach them that they should honour us. We must also live in such a way that makes it easy for them to do that. We too must live honourable lives.

When it is all said and done; how will your teenage child describe the impact you had on them? Paint that picture in your head and decide now, who you have to become and what you will have to do for that picture to be a reality.

If you are looking for a place to start, parents, I say start there!

CHAPTER 7 REFLECTION

What desirable behaviors has your teenager displayed that you know they picked up from you?

_____
_____
_____
_____
_____

What undesirable behaviors has your teenager displayed that you know they picked up from you?

_____
_____
_____
_____
_____

What is your understanding of the hidden curriculum? Do you believe it applies to your parenting journey?

_____
_____
_____
_____

What decisions have you made after reading this chapter?

DECSION 1

_____
_____

DECSION 2

_____
_____

DECSION 3

_____
_____

DECSION 4

_____
_____

DECSION 5

_____
_____

CHAPTER 8
HOW WILL YOU FIGHT?

✓ What's in your parent toolkit?

Parent Tool #1 - Prayer

Parents, your best fighting position will be on your knees. Get on your knees and hold your position. If you do not believe me, just ask my mother! In the times when I was acting out as a teenager and was out of control, my mother had all of Tarrant Baptist Church praying for me. Get some trusted prayer partners to pray about the following:

A CLEAR vision and direction for your teenager's life.

Their friends and associates. Ask God to align them with people who can help with accomplishing His vision for their lives.

Parent Tool #2 - Passion

Many parents make parenting decisions based on a need for approval (from other people), rather than being driven by the passion and purpose of their child. As a parent, tap into what drives YOUR child. Academics is very important, but parents, pay close attention to their passion; what truly drives them. There is absolutely nothing wrong with your child being a lawyer who is passionate about baking; a nurse who is passionate about singing; an engineer who loves telling jokes and does stand-up comedy, because that's what he is passionate about. It is important that we do not provoke our children by consistently forcing them to do something because it will look good to others or to avoid embarrassment for us.

Of course, as parents we must counsel our children wisely as to the consequences of their choosing one thing versus another. What we should not do is force them into something to suit our selfish agendas. We should not pressure our children based on questions like, how will it look? Or what will people say? We should encourage our children to be purpose-filled, always favouring what God says about them as opposed to what people think they should be.

Parent Tool #3 - Purpose

When I was a teenager, I never heard the word purpose. In speaking with my teenage students, they ask profound questions such as, "Mrs. Gray, do you think I was born for a reason?" which shows they are searching for something deeper than we are telling them. In essence, they are purpose questions. As a parent, essentially, we should help our teenagers uncover their purpose in life. We can then help them align their purpose with their profession. I believe this balance is very important.

Parents, how many times did you hear, "Go to school and get a good education. Settle down, get a stable job, get married and have children. Buy a house and everything will be okay." And let me make a very clear disclaimer again parents, I value higher education, I have a master's degree, I value family as I am married with two children. All I am saying is this, there is something a little deeper inside your teenager. The part we seldom talk about. The purpose that rests deep within their hearts and the purpose that rests deep within their souls.

If we do not help them to carefully and skilfully balance profession with purpose, they will ultimately get to a place where working a 9 to 5 job alone will not be able to satisfy their inner man. I know you have all heard about teenagers forced into starting a course of study in college that they did not want to do but their parents said was best for them, only for the child to drop out of college because they are stressed out. They have no interest in the major that was selected by, guess whom? Their parents. We have all been created to do something specific; a vessel commissioned to give service in some special way. Of all the 7.5 billion people on the planet, your teenage son or daughter is the only one sent to **do that thing, in that way**. I think it is worth exploring and nurturing.

Parent Tool #4 - Peace

Parents, I wanted to leave this tool for last. I need to point out here that I believe in discipline. I believe that some children, including teenagers, require good and stern correction. I do not believe in sparing the rod and spoiling the child. Noting here that the rod does not always have to be a physical one. There are many impactful ways to discipline teenagers without beating them.

For many parents, spanking can feel like the fastest and most effective way to change a child's behaviour. It often works in the short-term, but studies show corporal punishment has long-term consequences for children and, in particular, may not be the most effective method for teenagers. If you are looking for alternatives to corporal punishment, you may try the following:

Taking Away Privileges

Beating will cause physical pain and hurt a child for a minute or two but taking away privileges will hurt longer, and will possibly cause a child to self-correct. Take away the TV and video games and your teenager will have a reminder not to repeat that mistake. Usually three to five days is long enough to teach a teenager to learn from his/her mistake.

Engage In Upskilling (Equip & Teach)

One of the main problems with beating/corporal punishment is that it does not teach your child how to behave better. Coach your teenager by having open, honest but stern dialogue and provide concrete examples of what you expect of them the next time a situation arises. Teach them what a more appropriate response would be. Teenagers benefit from learning how to problem-solve, manage their emotions and compromise. When parents teach these skills, it can greatly reduce behaviour problems. Use discipline that is aimed at teaching, not punishing.

Praise Good Behaviour

As parents, we are quick to punish and not quick to praise. Help prevent behaviour problems by catching your teen being good. For example, when your teenager voluntarily comes home and starts studying for an exam/test, use the opportunity to comment by saying something like, "You are doing such a good job demonstrating how responsible you are. I appreciate that you took the initiative to study without me having to say anything, GOOD JOB!"

Show Consistent Love And Respect

Everyone wants to be loved, respected, liked and accepted, including your teenager. Be consistent in your display of affection. It does help.

In closing, I would like to highlight that this book has not been designed to give teenagers a free pass on bad behaviour and poor choices. The main purpose was to open your mind to a new approach; a new way of thinking. A new mindset about what will yield the desired results. Once you have carefully balanced correction and discipline with love, I believe you can be at peace.

Raise your child to have a palate for the things of God. Pray for them, work with them, collaborate with them and help them create a vision for their lives that aligns with God's purpose for their lives, then leave the rest to God. We cannot be with them every minute of every day. Ultimately, we cannot choose for them all the time either. And in the end, irrespective of how well we raise them, they will have to make their own choices.

What we can do is pray for them, cover them and raise them in the WAY they should go. God's promise is that they will not depart from it. It is a PROMISE and we must hold on to the promise even when things do not look like they will lead to a positive place. Do your part and hold on to the promise. I am living proof.

Chapter 8 Reflection

What did you learn from this chapter?

_____
_____
_____
_____
_____

How do you currently discipline your teenage child?

_____
_____
_____
_____
_____

Do you believe corporal punishment is the best way to change behaviour in your teenage son or daughter? Why or Why not?

_____
_____
_____
_____
_____

Which alternative method highlighted in this chapter will you use going forward?

_____

_____

_____

_____

_____

Parent Declaration Statement

Make this declaration every morning and every night until it becomes a part of you.

I _____, declare that I am committed to my parenting journey. I declare that I will love, protect and train up _____ in the way that he/she should go, understanding that _____ bears the very image of God. I will not provoke _____ to anger but bring him/her up in the instruction of the Lord, because this is what God requires of me.

Additional Copies

Of The

Individualized Success Plan (ISP)

INDIVIDUALIZED SUCCESS PLAN (ISP)

Name: _____

Age: _____

OVERALL VISION

Goals	Action Steps	Resources Needed	Persons Responsible	Timeline

INDIVIDUALIZED SUCCESS PLAN (ISP)

Name: _____

Age: _____

OVERALL VISION

Goals	Action Steps	Resources Needed	Persons Responsible	Timeline

INDIVIDUALIZED SUCCESS PLAN (ISP)

Name: _____

Age: _____

OVERALL VISION

Goals	Action Steps	Resources Needed	Persons Responsible	Timeline

INDIVIDUALIZED SUCCESS PLAN (ISP)

Name: _____

Age: _____

OVERALL VISION

Goals	Action Steps	Resources Needed	Persons Responsible	Timeline

INDIVIDUALIZED SUCCESS PLAN (ISP)

Name: _____

Age: _____

OVERALL VISION

Goals	Action Steps	Resources Needed	Persons Responsible	Timeline

INDIVIDUALIZED SUCCESS PLAN (ISP)

Name: _____

Age: _____

OVERALL VISION

Goals	Action Steps	Resources Needed	Persons Responsible	Timeline

INDIVIDUALIZED SUCCESS PLAN (ISP)

Name: _____

Age: _____

OVERALL VISION

Goals	Action Steps	Resources Needed	Persons Responsible	Timeline

INDIVIDUALIZED SUCCESS PLAN (ISP)

Name: _____

Age: _____

OVERALL VISION

Goals	Action Steps	Resources Needed	Persons Responsible	Timeline

INDIVIDUALIZED SUCCESS PLAN (ISP)

Name: _____

Age: _____

OVERALL VISION

Goals	Action Steps	Resources Needed	Persons Responsible	Timeline

INDIVIDUALIZED SUCCESS PLAN (ISP)

Name: _____

Age: _____

OVERALL VISION

Goals	Action Steps	Resources Needed	Persons Responsible	Timeline

INDIVIDUALIZED SUCCESS PLAN (ISP)

Name: _____

Age: _____

OVERALL VISION

Goals	Action Steps	Resources Needed	Persons Responsible	Timeline

INDIVIDUALIZED SUCCESS PLAN (ISP)

Name: _____

Age: _____

OVERALL VISION

Goals	Action Steps	Resources Needed	Persons Responsible	Timeline

INDIVIDUALIZED SUCCESS PLAN (ISP)

Name: _____

Age: _____

OVERALL VISION

Goals	Action Steps	Resources Needed	Persons Responsible	Timeline

INDIVIDUALIZED SUCCESS PLAN (ISP)

Name: _____

Age: _____

OVERALL VISION

Goals	Action Steps	Resources Needed	Persons Responsible	Timeline

INDIVIDUALIZED SUCCESS PLAN (ISP)

Name: _____

Age: _____

OVERALL VISION

Goals	Action Steps	Resources Needed	Persons Responsible	Timeline

INDIVIDUALIZED SUCCESS PLAN (ISP)

Name: _____

Age: _____

OVERALL VISION

Goals	Action Steps	Resources Needed	Persons Responsible	Timeline

INDIVIDUALIZED SUCCESS PLAN (ISP)

Name: _____

Age: _____

OVERALL VISION

Goals	Action Steps	Resources Needed	Persons Responsible	Timeline

INDIVIDUALIZED SUCCESS PLAN (ISP)

Name: _____

Age: _____

OVERALL VISION

Goals	Action Steps	Resources Needed	Persons Responsible	Timeline

INDIVIDUALIZED SUCCESS PLAN (ISP)

Name: _____

Age: _____

OVERALL VISION

Goals	Action Steps	Resources Needed	Persons Responsible	Timeline

INDIVIDUALIZED SUCCESS PLAN (ISP)

Name: _____

Age: _____

OVERALL VISION

Goals	Action Steps	Resources Needed	Persons Responsible	Timeline

SallyAnn Gray

RELATIONAL
RELEVANT
RIVETING

- @sallyannspeaks
- @sallyannspeaks
- SallyAnn Gray
- SallyAnn Gray

NSA NATIONAL SPEAKERS ASSOCIATION PROFESSIONAL MEMBER

SALLYANNGRAYSPEAKS.COM

"Shifting Mindsets Tranforming Lives"

RELEVANT.RELATIONAL.RIVETING

SallyAnn Gray is a professional member of the National Speakers Association. As an award-winning Author, Educational Consultant, Special Education Trained Teacher, Entrepreneur, International Speaker, Public Speaking Trainer, Wife and Mother, SallyAnn does it all! How? By being intentional about saying NO to the things that do not align with her core mission in life.

She has engaged thousands of teachers, teenagers, parents and corporate groups in high impact speeches, workshops and seminars and is one of the most requested speakers in Jamaica. She holds a Master's degree in Educational Leadership from Virginia Commonwealth University and has a Bachelor's degree in Special Education from the University of the West Indies. SallyAnn was nominated and won the Indie Legacy Author of the Year Award, for her first book, The Renewal: Revive Everything Necessary Empower Within. An honour she received in Baltimore, Maryland in June 2019.

WWW.SALLYANNGRAYSPEAKS.COM

"Shifting Mindsets Tranforming Lives"

At just 20 years old, SallyAnn was awarded the Jamaica Association of the Deaf Shield, for best performance in Education, upon her graduation from the Mico University College. SallyAnn has taught in Jamaica & the United States. She boasts a flourishing career as an educational consultant, where she focuses on the development of teachers, teenagers and parents, by finding solutions to social problems. SallyAnn's mission is to shift the mindset of teenagers globally, so they can transform their own lives. She has recognized in her work, that in order to develop youth, she must also focus on positive parenting. Her most recent book, 'Wayward Teen to Transformed Queen: Strategies to Help your Teenager Succeed' is a manual for parents of teenagers.

SallyAnn has written curriculum for the National Training Agency of Jamaica and is also a school inspector with the National Education Inspectorate of Jamaica. In her last professional role, she was Head of School & Programs Director for the TGL School of Sales & Sales Management.

SallyAnn is the founder of Global Speakers, an organization dedicated to training and developing emerging speakers to create global impact, using the power of their story. Given away by her mother at three months old, diagnosed with Attention Deficit Hyperactivity Disorder (ADHD) at fifteen years old and kicked out of high school at the age of seventeen, SallyAnn is no stranger to adversity. Her mantra is this "Anything is possible for him who believes. I don't think limits!"

Her Philosophy is simple

"I REMAIN COMMITTED TO GROWTH IN ALL AREAS OF MY LIFE. WHEN I GROW, I GROW OTHERS."

SALLY'S SIGNATURE PRESENTATIONS

MINDSET MASTERY THAT MOVES MOUNTAINS

Format: 60-90-minute keynote (Can be customized)

This program is perfect for:
- Corporate teams who require a productivity boost and inspiration
- Associations required to fulfil a huge mandate
- School administrators & teachers at the beginning of a School Year or a new term

GET ROOTED! GET PLANTED! GET GOING!

Format: 60 minute keynote (Can be customized)

This program is perfect for:
- Teenage boys & girls in school settings
- Teenage boys & girls at youth retreats & youth conferences
- At Risk Youth in Juvenile, Detention & Remand Center

LOVE, LEARN, TEACH & INCREASE

Format: 2-hour keynote/seminar/breakout session (Can be customized)

This program is perfect for:
- General Education Teachers in Secondary Institutions
- Special Education Teachers in Secondary Institutions
- Student teachers (Education Preparation Programs at the Secondary Level)

THE POWER OF POSITIVE PARENTING

Format: 60-90-minute keynote (Can be customized)

This program is perfect for:
- Parents of Teenagers
- Parents of At-Risk-Youth

For additional information on SallyAnn's NSA profile, visit the logo below:

https://www.espeakers.com/s/nsas/profile/40620?btsc=1

WWW.SALLYANNGRAYSPEAKS.COM

AREAS OF EXPERTISE

SALLYANN SPEAKS ON

MINDSET RENEWAL IN THE AREAS OF:

1. **PERSONAL DEVELOPMENT**
2. **PARENTING**
3. **PURPOSE**
4. **PUBLIC SPEAKING**

Sally's only reason for speaking, training and teaching people, is to stimulate and develop human potential. She delivers relevant, relational and riveting messages that fosters a shift in mindset. She creates and delivers keynote presentations and workshops to teachers, parents, teenagers and corporate groups, equipping them to leave mediocrity behind and step into excellence.

What's the best way to get started with your mindset revolution? One way is to identify where you may have fixed tendencies so that you can work to become more growth minded. We all live on a continuum, and consistent self-assessment helps us become the person we want to be.

WWW.SALLYANNGRAYSPEAKS.COM

AREAS OF EXPERTISE

Mindset renewal is an inquiry into the power of our beliefs, both conscious and unconscious, and how changing even the simplest of them can have profound impact on nearly every aspect of our lives. A "fixed mindset" assumes that our character, intelligence, and creative ability are static givens which we can't change in any meaningful way. A "growth mindset," on the other hand, thrives on challenge and sees failure not as evidence of unintelligence but as a heartening springboard for growth and for stretching our existing abilities. Out of these two mindsets, which we manifest from a very early age, springs a great deal of our behaviour, our relationship with success and failure in both professional and personal contexts, and ultimately our capacity to lead fulfilled lives.

Begin your journey of growth today.

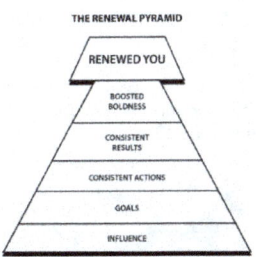

Diagram by SallyAnn Gray
Excerpt from 'The Renewal'

WWW.SALLYANNGRAYSPEAKS.COM

GLOBALLY REQUESTED SPEAKER

From international conference stages to schools, churches and corporate companies, SallyAnn creates customized presentations that meets the needs of an audience. An effective communicator and curriculum designer, SallyAnn crafts presentations that speaks to the bottom-line strategic objectives of organizations. She delivers the presentation in such a way, that it shifts the mindset of the audience. Whether she speaks to corporate groups, teachers, parents or teenagers, the result is the same 'A SHIFT IN MINDSET' which will transform lives.

SallyAnn is one of the most requested speakers in Jamaica and has delivered keynote presentations to government agencies, corporate entities and schools across the island.

WWW.SALLYANNGRAYSPEAKS.COM

Her most popular keynotes are:

- Positive parenting:
  Strategies to help your teen succeed
- The power of a transformed mind:
  Tips for creating a growth mindset
- Change your story, change your life
  The message of you, how to create global impact

BOOK SALLYANN TO SPEAK!

info@sallyanngrayspeaks.com

+1 876-838-8440 Makeda Laylor, Manager

WWW.SALLYANNGRAYSPEAKS.COM

A poor mindset will rob anyone of the life they deserve!

In her debut book, SallyAnn bravely shares how being adopted and diagnosed with ADHD caused her to develop a poor mindset. Her poor mindset plagued her during much of her adult life, despite external success. In this honest self-reflection of her most stressful moments, SallyAnn chronicles the steps she has taken to shift her mindset.

SallyAnn now thrives on a growth mindset and has developed a formula for daily mind renewal. She offers this formula to executives, teachers, parents and teenagers to stop the self-sabotage and embrace who they have been called to be.

SALLYANN GRAY HELPS PARENTS TO SHIFT THEIR MINDSET ON PARENTING

"When its all said and done, as parents, we all want well rounded, well adjusted contributing members of society as our offspring. In the end, it won't matter so much what their profession is: lawyer, doctor, Indian or chief. What will matter most is WHO they are." Whether you believe it or not parents, whether you embrace it or not, we have a HUGE role to play in that. Let us lead them not only in words but in deeds. For what we do will have a much bigger impact than what we say."

Excerpt, Wayward Teen to Transformed Queen:

ARE YOU PLANTED IN PURPOSE? SALLYANN WILL SHIFT YOUR MINDSET WHEN IT COMES TO PURPOSE!

Many in fact do start, but what does it take to remain consistent and finish your course? How do you remain rooted when life knocks you down? Is there a way to keep your focus despite the worries of life? Are the limits we see even real or are they self-imposed bars?

WWW.SALLYANNGRAYSPEAKS.COM

GOVERNMENT AGENCIES THAT HAVE WORKED WITH SALLY

SCHOOLS & UNIVERSITIES THAT HAVE WORKED WITH SALLY

COMPANIES THAT HAVE WORKED WITH SALLY

WHAT PEOPLE HAVE TO SAY

In just one moment with SallyAnn Gray, she inspired and invigorated my spirit! It is like oxygen to hear from her as she breathes words of encouragement to uplift me on this journey of life. She served as a panelist at my Premium Business Networking Signature Forum and she did not disappoint. Every person in the room left feeling inspired and empowered to take some serious action in their own life. The tips she shared on developing a growth mindset are practical and gave members of the audience great insight on how to make some immediate changes. We are looking forward to working with her again.

Erica McKenzie,
President & CEO, Creative Brands & Concepts- Jamaica

From the moment she opened her mouth, SallyAnn riveted the audience with her sense of humor. Her speech was impactful to say the least. She gave us practical tools we could implement immediately to develop a growth mindset. SallyAnn is a dynamic speaker and has the ability to help audiences dig deeper as they look for greater achievement in their careers and lives.

Paul Bryan,
Managing Director, Think Grow Lead-Training Masters

This lady needs no introduction. I am positive she will change the world with her powerful story. She was funny, witty, informative, inspiring and empowering. The questions SallyAnn asked the audience as she delivered her presentation caused us to pause, think and become reflective to the deeper calling we all have as human beings. Without hesitation, I highly recommend SallyAnn to any conference organizer seeking to inspire their audience to pursue greatness.

Jill Primm,
Founder, Restore Women's Conference- California

SallyAnn isn't your typical keynote speaker!
With her dynamic and interactive style,
she moves her audience into action by
giving strategies to renew their mind and create bottom line results!

WHY HIRE SALLY?

SallyAnn will partner with you to achieve the objectives of your event.
She has two main goals:
1) Make YOU, the event planner SHINE!
2) Give your attendees powerful
and practical content they can
take action on NOW!

www.ingramcontent.com/pod-product-compliance
Lightning Source LLC
Chambersburg PA
CBHW052148110526
44591CB00012B/1894